"We never get beyond the message of the cross. C.J. Mahaney applies this truth in a powerful but winsome way. It is a book for *every* Christian, and I'm delighted to recommend it."

"Again and again, by his life and writing, C.J. Mahaney has summoned me to the centrality of the cross. I love Christ more because of this precious ministry."

"Every Timothy needs a Paul. C.J. Mahaney is mine…and this book contains his life-message. It is *my* handbook for pursuing a cross centered life. Read it yourself, and let God realign your life."

"My friend C. J. Mahaney has a passion for Jesus and his people. He lives the cross centered life and is therefore qualified to talk about it. Let C.J. walk you through the transforming power of the gospel. You'll be refreshed…and deeply thankful for God's grace."

"This biblical, practical book written by a wise and godly man helped me, as it will help others, in overcoming harmful patterns of thinking about our daily lives as Christians and in focusing on the finished work of Christ on the cross."

THE CROSS CENTERED LIFE

LIFECHANGE BOOKS

C.J. MAHANEY

WITH KEVIN MEATH

Multnomah® Publishers *Sisters, Oregon*

THE CROSS CENTERED LIFE

published by Multnomah Publishers, Inc.

© 2002 by Sovereign Grace Ministries

International Standard Book Number: 1-59052-045-9

Cover image by Ellen Carey/Photonica

Unless otherwise indicated, Scripture quotations are from:
The Holy Bible, New International Version © 1973, 1984 by International
Bible Society, used by permission of Zondervan Publishing House

Other Scripture quotations:
The Holy Bible, English Standard Version (ESV) © 2001 by Crossway Bibles,
a division of Good News Publishers. Used by permission. All rights reserved.

Multnomah is a trademark of Multnomah Publishers, Inc.,
and is registered in the U.S. Patent and Trademark Office.
The colophon is a trademark of Multnomah Publishers, Inc.

Printed in the United States of America

For information:

MULTNOMAH PUBLISHERS, INC.•POST OFFICE BOX 1720•SISTERS, OREGON 97759

Library of Congress Cataloging-in-Publication Data

Mahaney, C. J.
    The cross-centered life / by C.J. Mahaney with Kevin Meath.
        p. cm.
Includes bibliographical references.
    ISBN 1-59052-045-9
    1. Christian life. I. Meath, Kevin. II. Title.
    BV4501.3 .M24 2002
    248.4--dc21   2002007724

05 06 07 08 09—12 11 10 9

To Carolyn

Apart from the Savior,
I've received no greater gift from God
than your love.

Behold, you are beautiful, my love,
behold, you are beautiful!
You have captivated my heart, my sister, my bride.

SONG OF SOLOMON 4:1, 9 (ESV)

CONTENTS

One

RESTATING
THE OBVIOUS

The Most Important Truth Is the Easiest to Forget

TIMOTHY'S HANDS TREMBLED as he read. He almost cradled the letter, as though his gentleness with the parchment would somehow be conveyed to its author, now chained in a cold Roman dungeon.

The letter came from the apostle Paul; it would be his last.

For years Timothy had pushed the thought of losing Paul out of his mind. Paul had been like a father. A friend and mentor who guided and instructed the young pastor. How could he minister without Paul's reassuring words,

his confidence, his prayers? But now, Timothy knew
Paul's death was imminent.

"I am already being poured out like a drink offer-
ing," Paul wrote, "and the time has come for my depar-
ture" (2 Timothy 4:6).

Timothy read the closing lines of the letter through
his tears. But then he stopped and pushed them away
abruptly. How could he wallow in grief when his old
friend faced death so boldly?

He could almost hear the voice of Paul through the
words on the page: "Keep your head in all situations,
endure hardship...discharge all the duties of your ministry" (2 Timothy 4:5).

Now Timothy began to read the letter again. He read
slowly, deliberately. His eyes bored into each word, each
sentence. In the closing moments of Paul's life, would
God give him a flash of insight that he would pass on to
Timothy? Paul was the apostle to the Gentiles, a man
who had been swept up into heaven itself (see 2
Corinthians 12:2–4). What special insight, like a long
forgotten key, would he now reveal?

As Timothy read, heart pounding, the truth—the
key—hit him with piercing clarity. He saw more clearly
than ever what Paul had given his life to—and for which
Timothy, too, would spend himself.

The message of Paul's final letter revealed no new

truth, no hidden knowledge, just "one truth" he had given his life to spread. *The good news. The news of the cross.*

And now the letter, which at first reading had been to Timothy the obituary of his dearest friend, became a joy-filled, bold restatement of all Paul had lived for, and all he would soon die for.

"Of this gospel I was appointed a herald and an apostle and a teacher.... I am not ashamed, because I know whom I have believed" (2 Timothy 1:11–12).

The words seemed to shout from the page: "What you heard from me, keep as the pattern of sound teaching, with faith and love in Christ Jesus" (2 Timothy 1:13).

Timothy could almost see Paul's fiery eyes blazing into his own, feel his gnarled fingers gripping his arm. "Guard the good deposit that was entrusted to you— guard it with the help of the Holy Spirit who lives in us" (2 Timothy 1:14).

You don't need a new truth, he heard his old friend saying. Guard the *one* truth. Keep the *one* message.

"Remember Jesus Christ, raised from the dead, descended from David. This is my gospel" (2 Timothy 2:8).

THE MESSAGE

The apostle Paul recognized the universal danger of forgetting what is most important. He refused to be pulled away from the gospel.

The cross was the centerpiece of Paul's theology. It wasn't merely *one* of Paul's messages; it was *the* message. He taught about other things as well, but whatever he taught was always derived from, and related to, the foundational reality that *Jesus Christ died so that sinners would be reconciled to God and forgiven by God.*

Theologian D. A. Carson writes of Paul, "He cannot long talk about Christian joy, or Christian ethics, or Christian fellowship, or the Christian doctrine of God, or anything else, without finally tying it to the cross. Paul is gospel-centered; he is cross centered."[1]

From his first epistle to his final letter to Timothy, Paul kept the atoning death and resurrection of Jesus at the center of his teaching. He "resolved to know nothing...except Jesus Christ and him crucified" (1 Corinthians 2:2).

And this wasn't a cold theological formula, either. Paul lived a cross centered life because the cross had saved and transformed his own life.

Writing thirty years after his conversion, Paul's memory of what he had once been, and what God had done for him, remained at the forefront of his mind. "Even though I was once a blasphemer and a persecutor and a violent man," he wrote Timothy, "I was shown mercy" (1 Timothy 1:13).

NEVER FORGET

I can relate to Paul's amazement at being shown mercy. I've lived in the same part of Maryland since I was a boy. Hardly a month goes by that I'm not reminded of who I once was.

Before God saved me in 1972, I, too, was a blasphemer. I lived for myself and my own pleasure. I lived in rebellion against God and mocked those who followed Him. I spent my high school and college years deeply immersed in the local drug culture.

Sometimes, late at night, my friends and I would seek out quiet, isolated places where we could come down safely from drug highs. On more than a few occasions it was a D.C. monument. Other times a peaceful street under thick, deep trees. Or even the terminal at what was then a little-used airport called Dulles, where the doors stayed open long after the day's flights had ceased and we could move through the nearly deserted canyon of a building.

Someday soon I'll be near one of those places again,

and the memories will flood back in. I'll remember what I once was, and be reminded of what I now am.

Often my eyes fill with tears at the memories of my foolishness and sin. And in the same instant, my heart will be filled with an unspeakable, holy joy. I am no longer the same! By the finished work of Jesus Christ on the cross, I've been forgiven of the countless sins I've committed.

"Blessed is the man," David wrote, "whose sin the LORD does not count against him" (Psalm 32:2). This truth echoes through my soul, resonating in places far deeper than any drug can go.

Many people today try to run from the past. I suppose I could try to as well, by leaving the hometown that holds so many reminders of my sinfulness. But I consider living here a gift from God. The regular reminders of my past are precious to me.

Why? Because, like Paul, I never want to forget the great mercy shown me.

WE ALL NEED THIS

If you're a Christian, you don't need to live in the same place all your life to remember who you once were. And you don't need a background in drugs, or any other dramatic conversion experience, for the cross to be dear to you.

Regardless of our pasts, we've all sinned and fallen short of God's glory (Romans 3:23). My nine-year-old son Chad's life is very different from mine. He's being raised in a Christian home. He has been taught God's Word. And unlike his father, he is surrounded by people in a local church who respect godliness and humility, not worldliness and pride.

But as Chad enters young adulthood, the most important thing I can teach him is that, even though he's being raised in a Christian family and is leading a moral life, he's a sinner who desperately needs the substitutionary death of Christ to be forgiven by God.

And so I'm teaching him the gospel, day by day. I tell him that he's a sinner just like his dad, and that sin is a serious problem. I put it in words that his young mind can understand, but I don't ignore or minimize the seriousness of sin. Through his actions and attitudes he has rebelled against his Maker. And this great God is perfectly holy and must respond with fierce opposition to sin. He must punish it.

Some might find it surprising that I would teach a nine-year-old about God's wrath toward sin. But I find it surprising that any loving person would withhold this truth from another person they love. Because only when we understand God's wrath toward sin can we realize that we need to be saved from it. Only when we hear the very bad news that we're deserving of judgment can we appreciate the very good news that God has provided salvation through His Son.

And this is what I hold out to my young son as the hope of his life: that Jesus, God's perfect, righteous Son, died in his place for his sins. Jesus took all the punishment; Jesus received all the wrath as He hung on the cross, so people like Chad and his sinful daddy could be completely forgiven.

THE ONLY ESSENTIAL MESSAGE

I hope to teach my son many other things as well, but the gospel is the one essential thing for him to know.

"The gospel," writes Jerry Bridges, "is not only the most important message in all of history; it is the *only* essential message in all of history. Yet we allow thousands of professing Christians to live their entire lives without clearly understanding it and experiencing the joy of living by it."[2]

Author John Stott agrees. "All around us we see Christians and churches relaxing their grasp on the gospel, fumbling it, and in danger of letting it drop from their hands altogether."[3]

Sometimes the most obvious truths are the ones we need to be reminded of the most.

George Orwell once noted that "sometimes the first duty of intelligent men is the restatement of the obvious."[4] Perhaps the purpose of this book is to restate the obvious, yet oft-neglected, truth of the gospel, to bring it before you one more time.

On the other hand, maybe you're thinking, "I already know this truth—I've known it for years." That's good, but let me ask you this:

Is your life cross centered?

The symptoms that arise from *not* being cross centered are easy to spot. Do any of these describe you?

- You often lack joy.
- You're not consistently growing in spiritual maturity.
- Your love for God lacks passion.
- You're always looking for some new technique, some "new truth" or new experience that will pull all the pieces of your faith together.

If you can relate to any of these symptoms, let me encourage you to keep reading. As you learn to live a cross centered life, you'll learn:

- How to break free from joy-robbing, legalistic thinking and living

- How to leave behind the crippling effects of guilt and condemnation
- How to stop basing your faith on your emotions and circumstances
- How to grow in gratefulness, joy, and holiness

These aren't the overhyped promises of an author wanting to convince you to read his book. These are God's promises to all who respond to His wonderful plan of salvation.

Too many of us have moved on from that glorious plan. In our never-ending desire to move forward and make sure that everything we do, say, and think is relevant to modern living, too many of us have stopped concentrating on the wonders of Jesus crucified.

Too many of us have fumbled the most important truth of the Bible, and therefore we've suffered the consequences.

But it's not too late to change. It's not too late to restate and reestablish the obvious truth as the *most important truth in your life*.

The message that Paul had for Timothy is the same message God has for you. You need to rediscover the truth that first saved you. The key to joy, to growth, to passion isn't hiding from you. It's right before your eyes.

It's the gospel.

Two

WHAT'S YOUR LIFE
CENTERED ON?

Why the Cross Should Define Our Lives

ON MONDAY, ALICE BOUGHT A PARROT. It didn't talk, so the next day she returned to the pet store.

"He needs a ladder," she was told. She bought a ladder, but another day passed and the parrot still didn't say a word.

"How about a swing?" the clerk suggested.

So Alice bought a swing. The next day, a mirror. The next day, a miniature plastic tree. The next day, a shiny parrot toy. On Sunday morning, Alice was standing outside the pet store when it opened. She had the parrot cage in her hand and tears in her eyes. Her parrot was dead.

"Did it ever say a word?" the store owner asked.

"Yes," Alice said through her sobs. "Right before he died, he looked at me and asked, 'Don't they sell any food at that pet store?'"

THE MATTER OF FIRST IMPORTANCE

Many good causes and activities can occupy a Christian's time and attention. But just as no amount of parrot-cage amenities can make up for a lack of parrot food, nothing can replace the gospel in a Christian's life. Without it our souls will become like Alice's pet—starving in a crowded cage.

It's important to ask honestly what we're currently building our lives around. Before we can talk about how to live a cross centered life, we have to identify what our life is centered on right now. We're all living lives centered on *some*thing. But is it the *right* thing?

So think about this for a moment. What is the main thing in your life?

Let me put it another way. What are you most passionate about? What do you think about when you can think about whatever you want? What do you love to talk about?

What defines you?

Is it your career? A relationship you're in? Your hobby? Your political affiliation? A fascination with the latest electronic gadgets?

Or maybe your main thing is something that's clearly others centered. Maybe it's your ministry, your family. Maybe it's homeschooling, or a cause like the prolife movement. Good things, all, but not the *one thing* God says should be the most important—the matter of first importance.

"I want to remind you of the gospel I preached to you," Paul wrote. "For what I received I passed on to you as of first importance: that Christ died for our sins" (1 Corinthians 15:1, 3).

First importance. The Bible tells us that, while there are many different callings and many possible areas of service in the kingdom of God, *one transcendent truth* should define our lives. One simple truth should motivate our work and affect every part of who we are.

Christ died for our sins.

If there's anything in life that we should be passionate about, it's the gospel. And I don't mean passionate only about sharing it with others. I mean passionate in thinking about it, dwelling on it, rejoicing in it, allowing it to color the way we look at the world. Only one thing can be of first importance to each of us. And only the gospel ought to be.

THE NEW, THE BETTER...OR THE BEST?

Our culture is thoroughly saturated with advertising. Each day we're barraged with appeals for our attention. And every appeal claims in some way that it offers something new or better. Or both.

There's nothing wrong with being new or better. Our problem is that we have come to see these two adjectives as synonymous—as if anything new is always better, and if something is better it must be new.

Sadly, an obsession with new and better is as common inside the church as it is outside. The list is endless and always changing. Diet and health. Healing and miracles. Gifts of the Holy Spirit. Godly marriage. Creationism. Worship music. Evangelism. Missions. The return of the Lord. A specific form of liturgy.

You can find many sincere, mature Christians who have built their lives around each of these issues. Some even switch issues every few years, when something new or (presumably!) better captures their attention.

Please don't misunderstand. There's an important place for all these concerns. They shouldn't be neglected or ignored. But neither should we let any issue, topic, or cause displace the gospel from its rightful place at the very center of our lives.

D. A. Carson's concern is well justified when he writes, "I fear that the cross, without ever being disowned, is constantly in danger of being dismissed from the central place it must enjoy, by relatively peripheral insights that take on far too much weight. Whenever the periphery is in danger of displacing the center, we are not far removed from idolatry."[5]

New things will always come along. Some will be good; some will be better. But according to God, only one thing will ever be best.

He sent His Son into the world to live a perfect life and go to the cross to bear His wrath for sinners like you and me.

This is the "main thing," the very essence of the cross centered life. It was Paul's main thing. Nothing else—not even things that are biblical and honorable—are of equal or greater importance.

OUR DAILY CHALLENGE

And yet, every day we face the temptation to move away from the gospel. That's why this book talks so much about *what it takes to keep the gospel central*. We will look at three main tendencies that can draw our hearts away:

1. *Legalism,* which means basing our relationship with God on our own performance.
2. *Condemnation,* which means being more focused on our sin than on God's grace.
3. *Subjectivism,* which means basing our view of God on our changing feelings and emotions.

In the next three chapters, we'll examine each of these tendencies more closely and discover how we can overcome them. But as we saw in this chapter, the first and most important thing you can do—*always*—is to make sure the gospel is at the very center of your life.

What's of first importance to you? Whatever it is, you've probably been thinking about it as you've read. If it's something other than the gospel, are you willing to repent to God and reorder your life?

Whatever's of first importance to you might be a good thing. It might be a perfectly honorable, perfectly legitimate thing. And your life might be so wrapped up in it that you have trouble imagining it being of secondary importance.

Let me urge you to do whatever it takes to make the gospel your passion. Ask God to change your heart so that, like Paul said in Galatians 6:14, you can say, "May I never boast except in the cross of our Lord Jesus Christ."

Three

BREAKING THE
RULES OF LEGALISM

*How the Cross Rescues You
from the Performance Trap*

ONE OF THE GREATEST HINDRANCES to keeping the gospel central in our lives is our creeping tendency toward legalism. It's an age-old foe to God's plan of salvation through faith alone. From the earliest days of the church, legalism has thrown Christians off course and sidetracked them all over the place.

And it's just as active and destructive today as it ever was.

It's important to understand that a legalist isn't just someone with higher standards or more rules than you.

A lot of us wrongly stereotype a legalistic person as one who doesn't go to the movies, or who thinks that any music with a beat is evil. Legalism is much more subtle and serious than that.

Here's a simple definition that I use: *Legalism is seeking to achieve forgiveness from God and acceptance by God through obedience to God.*

In other words, a legalist is anyone who behaves as if they can earn God's approval and forgiveness through personal performance. Thomas Schreiner writes that "legalism has its origin in self-worship. If people are justified through their obedience to the law, then they merit praise, honor, and glory. Legalism, in other words, means the glory goes to people rather than God."[6]

Are you starting to see what a serious problem this is? Though we might never state any of its underlying assumptions in plain English, the implications of legalism are staggering in their arrogance. Legalism claims that the death of Jesus on the cross was either unnecessary or insufficient. It essentially says to God, "Your plan didn't work. The cross wasn't enough and I need to add my good works to it to be saved."

Of course, no Christian would dare utter such terrible words. But when we shift our concentration away from the gospel, legalism slowly and subtly twists our thinking until our lives make this awful statement on their own. They speak more plainly than words.

Do you know how to discern legalism in your life?

SPINNING PLATES

When I was a young boy in the 1960s, one of my favorite TV programs was the Ed Sullivan Show. It aired live on Sunday nights, and it was a mix of big-name performers, promising newcomers, and quirky novelty acts.

One of the more popular acts on the show provides a helpful picture of how legalism can hijack a Christian's life. I'm referring to the "Plate Spinner," who employed two kinds of objects—very thin, flexible rods that were close to seven feet long, and regular round, ceramic plates.

The plate spinner would stand a rod on end, hold a plate on top, and spin it with great force. The rod would stand nearly erect, with just a slight bow to it from the weight of the plate, which whirred furiously a foot or so above the spinner's head.

Then the spinner would set up a second rod-and-plate. Then a third. And soon the stage would be transformed into a small forest of plates, wiggling and swaying on their sticks.

By the time eight or ten plates were in motion, the first plate had begun to slow down and wobble danger-ously. The spinner would rush back over and, with remarkably skilled hands, instantly return the plate to top-speed rotation. Then he would be off to set up another rod-and-plate combination.

Eventually, so much was happening onstage that disaster seemed inevitable. As plates wobbled wildly all around him, the spinner would pretend not to notice, triggering thousands of us to shout desperately at our television sets. (At least, thousands was what I assumed—surely I wasn't the only one!)

But every time, at the last possible second, he would spring into action, running back and forth in a flurry of activity. Somehow he always got there in time.

A SPINNER NAMED STUART

Though it doesn't involve rods and plates, the life of a legalist can become just as frenetic as the plate spinner's performance.

Meet Stuart. He's a brand-new believer who has a lot to learn about the Christian life, but he has a genuine love for Jesus Christ. One Sunday morning during the church service, his friend Mike notices that Stuart has a little trouble finding the book of Romans. After the meeting, he asks Stuart if he's regularly reading his Bible.

"Uh, sure," Stuart replies. "There's so much there, I just look at different things."

Mike raises his eyebrows. "You're reading at random? That's really not the best way. You need to read the Word seriously! Listen, I have this schedule that tells you how to read the whole Bible in a year, a little every day. I'll make you a copy."

"Wow!" Stuart replies. "You mean by this time next year I could have read the entire Bible? That would be great!"

And so, just a few days later, Stuart places a single flexible rod onto the stage of his Christian life, lifts up a plate called Bible Reading, and spins it hard. And it stays in place!

Now let's fast-forward about six months. Stuart is now much, much busier than ever before in his life. After Mike told him about the importance of Bible reading, Jimmy encouraged him to meditate on Scripture. A few days later, Andrew extolled the glories of attending a weekly accountability meeting with guys from the church. In a sermon, his pastor emphasized the importance of church prayer meetings.

Then Stuart attended a conference on evangelism. He needed to be witnessing every day. Then he heard a radio program about fasting, and another about personal holiness.

One by one, Stuart added more and more spiritual activities to his life. Each was good. Some were vital. Yet without realizing it, Stuart allowed a dangerous shift to take place in his mind and heart. What God had intended to be a means of experiencing grace, Stuart had changed into a means of earning grace. Instead of being a further expression of his confidence in God's saving work in his life, his spiritual activities became spinning plates to maintain.

The shift is plainly seen on Sunday mornings. On one Sunday, Stuart sings and praises God with evident sincerity and zeal. Why? Because he's just had a really good week. Not a single plate has wobbled.

But on another Sunday, following a week in which several plates fell, Stuart is hesitant to approach God. He finds it difficult to worship freely, because he feels that God disapproves of him. His confidence is no longer in the gospel; it's in his own performance, which hasn't been so great lately.

Can you relate to Stuart's mistake? Do you see signs of legalism in your own life? Do you often find that you're more aware of your sin than of what Jesus accomplished at the cross? When you picture God's attitude toward you, do you think of God as disappointed with you rather than delighting over you?

Do you lack holy joy? Do you look to your "spinning plates" for the confidence—indeed, even the right—to approach God? If you answer yes to any of these questions, you've probably begun to live under the rules of legalism.

But don't let this discourage you. God wants to rescue you from the futility of plate spinning. Let's examine how a right understanding of the gospel can free us from the joyless restrictions of legalism.

JUSTIFIED: THE FINISHED WORK

In case you're wondering, breaking free from legalism doesn't mean you stop reading your Bible, praying, or sharing the gospel. If you and I want to grow in our faith, we need to take advantage of the tools God gives us in these important spiritual pursuits. The issue is our motive and our understanding of what it means to be saved by grace.

Remember what happened the day you first repented of your sins and trusted in Jesus Christ? Romans 3:26 says that, in that moment, you were justified, or declared righteous, before God.

That word *justified* is important. It refers to your status before God. When you put your faith in Jesus, God, the judge, hands down the verdict that you are righteous. He transfers the perfect, sinless record of Jesus to you.

This is amazing grace at its most amazing. In the moment that you first believed, your past sin didn't cease to exist. You hadn't done any good work that could somehow make up for your disobedience.

Yet God completely and totally forgave you. He not only wiped the record of your sin away, he credited the righteousness of His Son to you.

SANCTIFIED: THE ONGOING WORK

However, the power of the gospel doesn't end when we're justified. When God declares a sinner righteous, He immediately begins the process of making that sinner more like His Son. Through the work of His Spirit, through the power of His word and fellowship with other believers, God peels away our desires for sin, renews our minds, and changes our lives. This ongoing work is what we call "sanctification."

Sanctification is a process—the process of becoming more like Christ, of growing in holiness. This process begins the instant you are converted and will not end until you meet Jesus face-to-face.

Sanctification is about our own choices and behavior. It involves work. Empowered by God's Spirit, we strive. We fight sin. We study Scripture and pray, even when we don't feel like it. We flee temptation. We press on; we run hard in the pursuit of holiness. And as we become more and more sanctified, the power of the gospel conforms us more and more closely, with ever-increasing clarity, to the image of Jesus Christ.

DON'T CONFUSE THE TWO

Do you have a clear grasp of what justification and sanctification are?

Without understanding the distinction between the two, you will be vulnerable to legalism. I encourage you to understand these theological terms, not so you can impress your friends, but because understanding the differences between justification and sanctification is vital to defeating legalism.

Nearly every man and woman I've met who has struggled with legalism has had a faulty understanding of how justification and sanctification are related to each other, and how they're distinct. We must distinguish between justifying grace and sanctifying grace, but never separate them.

At the risk of repeating myself, let me line them up next to each other so you can clearly see the differences between them:

- Justification is being *declared* righteous. Sanctification is being *made* righteous—being conformed to the image of Christ.
- Justification is our *position* before God. Sanctification is our *practice*. You don't practice justification! It happens once for all, upon conversion.

- Justification is objective—Christ's work *for* us. Sanctification is subjective—Christ's work *within* us.
- Justification is *immediate* and complete upon conversion. You will never be more justified than you are the first moment you trust in the Person and finished work of Christ. Sanctification is a *process*. You will be more sanctified as you continue in grace-motivated obedience.

William Plumer sums it up well when he writes, "Justification is an act. It is not a work, or a series of acts. It is not progressive. The weakest believer and the strongest saint are alike equally justified. Justification admits no degrees. A man is either wholly justified or wholly condemned in the sight of God."[7]

THE LEGALIST'S MISTAKE

So do you see the distinction? Now…here's the mistake the legalist makes. He confuses his own ongoing participation in the process of sanctification with God's finished work in justification.

In other words, he thinks that godly practices and good works somehow contribute to his justification. But God's Word is clear when it says, "Therefore no one will

be declared righteous in his sight by observing the law…"
(Romans 3:20). None of us earn God's approval and love
by our good works. None of us can add to the finished,
complete work of Jesus on the cross. He paid the price of
our sins. He satisfied God's wrath.

Our participation in the process of sanctification
comes only after we've been totally accepted and made
right before God through faith in Jesus. So yes, we work
hard at obeying God's word. We read our Bibles. We
pray. We meditate on Scripture. We memorize Scripture.
We share the gospel. We serve in our church. We fast.
God commands us in His Word to do many things, and
our obedience is both pleasing to Him and brings His
blessing to our lives.

But not one of these good spiritual activities adds to
our justification. We're never "more saved" or "more
loved" by God. Our work is motivated by the grace God
has poured out in our lives.

PUT DOWN YOUR PLATES

The mistake of a legalistic plate spinner like Stuart is that
he substitutes sanctification for justification. "Our greatest temptation and mistake," writes Sinclair Ferguson, "is
to try to smuggle character into God's work of grace."[8]
The legalist allows his performance of spiritual duties to

become his preoccupation and a source of self-righteous pride. In doing so, he unwittingly walks away from the main thing—the gospel.

I know the temptation to legalism. That's why, when I complete my daily devotions and close my Bible, I make a point of reminding myself that Jesus' work, not mine, is the basis of my forgiveness and acceptance by God.

"Lord, I ask for Your grace and strength as I seek to serve You today," I pray. "I thank You that all Your blessings flow to me from Your Son's work on my behalf. I am justified by Your grace alone. None of my efforts to obey You and grow in sanctification add to Your finished work at the cross."

What joy the gospel gives me. I can approach the throne of God with confidence. Not because I've done a good job at my spiritual duties, but because I'm clothed in the righteousness of Jesus Christ.

God wants you to have this same confidence. He's not impressed with your spinning plates. So renounce all self-righteousness. Make your boast the achievement and work of your substitute and Savior, Jesus Christ.

Four

UNLOADING CONDEMNATION

How the Cross Removes Guilt and Shame

I RARELY READ THE COMICS IN THE NEWSPAPER, but a few years ago someone showed me one I had to keep. It's from a strip called *Cathy*. Cathy appears to be a single woman in her thirties. In this particular cartoon she is sitting at home, alone with her thoughts.

Things I should have done at work, she thinks to herself. *Things I wish I'd said to Irving, things I promised myself to never do again but I did anyway. Ways I made myself miserable that I could have avoided.*

Her look of depression deepens.

Things I could have done for my family, my puppy, my friends, my coworkers, my neighbor, my finances, my home, my closets, my diet, and millions of people in need whom I've never met.

In the final frame, Cathy summarizes her plight. "Even when I'm not going anywhere, I have three hundred pounds of luggage with me."

CHECK YOUR BAGS

It's amazing how close to home a comic strip can strike. Like Cathy, we can all generate a depressing list of things undone, unsaid, and unaccomplished. Even when we're not going anywhere we can carry hundreds of pounds of luggage.

The Bible calls this luggage "condemnation." At one time or another we all find ourselves carrying some, whether big or small.

Condemnation appears in innumerable forms. It's the weight on the heart of the businessman who was rarely home when his kids were growing up. It's the undercurrent of grief and mental self-torture in the woman who had an abortion twelve years ago. It's the nagging conscience of the Christian man who muttered a crude insult at a reckless driver twelve minutes ago. It's the lingering sense of regret over a lack of prayer; it's kind words unsaid and promises broken.

Some of us have been carrying so much, for so long, that we think it's normal to go through life weighted down. And the truth is that, apart from the cross, condemnation *is* normal. Without Jesus, we all deserve to be condemned and punished for sin. But in Romans 8:1 the Bible tells us, "There is now no condemnation for those who are in Christ Jesus."

We don't have to go through life under condemnation. In this chapter I want to show you how to unload this crippling burden by embracing the forgiveness offered by the gospel.

LOW-GRADE GUILT

Condemnation is something we all deal with at one time or another. It comes in different degrees. It's a mistake to think that condemnation is a problem only for people who have committed "major" sins.

We can become condemned over any sin, past or present, great or small. The common element is a sustained sense of guilt or shame over sins for which you have repented to God and to any appropriate individuals.

Are you allowing condemnation into your own life? Ask yourself the following questions:

- Do you relate to God as if you were on a kind of permanent probation, suspecting that at any moment He may haul you back into the jail cell of His disfavor?
- When you come to worship do you maintain a "respectful distance" from God, as if He were a fascinating but ill-tempered celebrity known for lashing out at His fans?
- When you read Scripture does it reveal the boundless love of the Savior or merely intensify your condemnation?
- Are you more aware of your sin than you are of God's grace, given you through the cross?

Do you see any traces of condemnation in your life? Don't be surprised if you do. But don't keep carrying the burden! Because of the gospel's power you can be completely free of all condemnation.

Not mostly free; *completely* free.

Don't buy the lie that cultivating condemnation and wallowing in your shame is somehow pleasing to God, or that a constant, low-grade guilt will somehow promote holiness and spiritual maturity.

It's just the opposite! *God is glorified when we believe with all our hearts that those who trust in Christ can never be condemned.* It's only when we receive his free gift of grace and live in the good of total forgiveness that we're able to turn from old, sinful ways of living and walk in grace-motivated obedience.

AN UNINVITED GUEST

The Bible records the story of a very unusual dinner party that Jesus attended at the home of Simon the Pharisee. In this very tense and powerful scene, described in Luke 7:36–50, we're provided an important lesson about condemnation.

We're not told why Jesus was invited to this dinner, but we know tensions were high between Him and the Pharisees. His host had rudely and conspicuously withheld from Jesus all the basic social courtesies due a dinner guest: a kiss of greeting, washed feet, a drop of anointing oil. These glaring omissions were obvious to all present.

Then an unexpected person appears. Into the room comes a known prostitute, a woman despised by polite society.

What happens next is unthinkable to those watching. As Jesus reclines at the low table, leaning on one elbow, His feet stretched out away from the table, the woman stands over Him and begins to weep.

All conversation ceases.

The sound of her weeping grows in volume, filling

the house and spilling out into the street. Her freely flow-ing tears wet His unwashed feet. She kneels down, takes down her hair, and with it begins to wash Jesus' tear-stained feet. Then she kisses them and anoints them with perfume as an act of worship.

Can you feel the atmosphere in that room? No one eats. No one moves. Perhaps strangest of all, Jesus does nothing to suggest that the shocking behavior of this sin-ful woman is *anything but appropriate*.

OUR MANY SINS

I believe God recorded this dramatic event in Scripture for a very specific purpose. He wants us to see ourselves in that woman and follow her example.

The woman who washed Jesus' feet with her tears was someone who had repented of her sins. This isn't her first encounter with Jesus. No doubt she had listened to Him teach, and had found in His words the hope for for-giveness and cleansing no one else was willing to grant her.

When we meet her she has already believed in Jesus and turned away from her old life. This is not the account of her salvation; rather, this is a beautiful expression of Christian worship born of her love, adoration, and thankfulness toward her Savior. She recognizes her sin and unworthiness, and weeps deeply.

But here's what is so important for us to see. Her tears are not tears of condemnation. She weeps because her guilt is gone. She loves much because she's been forgiven much. These are tears of joy, gratitude, and extravagant devotion.

LOSE YOUR LUGGAGE

The Christian who desires to live a cross centered life will regularly face his or her own depravity and the seriousness of personal sin, squarely and unflinchingly. It's a reality. But the reality of the death and resurrection of Jesus for the forgiveness of sin is even greater.

This doesn't mean we won't struggle occasionally with condemnation.

On a daily basis, the luggage of condemnation will show up on our doorstep, just begging us to load it on our backs. In its opposition to God, our flesh will tell us that Jesus' sacrifice couldn't possibly be enough to win the Father's favor completely, unreservedly, and forever.

I mean—just look at all that luggage! The enemy of our soul with his lies will always be swift to whisper accusations. When these challenges come, don't try to fight condemnation by promising to pray more, or to fast more often, or to memorize more Scripture. Future obedience is certainly important. But it's impossible to resolve issues of yesterday by doing better tomorrow.

Our promises of future obedience, however sincere, do not resolve condemnation for past sin.

BEATING CONDEMNATION

Here's how to beat condemnation. Confess your sin to God. Then believe in Him. Exercise the gift of faith that God has given you to believe that Jesus died for the very sins you're being condemned for.

The punishment He received was for you. His resurrection is proof that God accepted Jesus' sacrifice. The sins of your past and the sin you just committed were all atoned for; you need carry their weight no more.

You can't do it. That's why Jesus did it for you.

Being freed from condemnation doesn't require that we forget or deny the depth and depravity of our sins, whether they're sins committed prior to our conversion or sins committed since our conversion. In fact, if we want to know the joy and gratitude that the woman at Jesus' feet experienced, we must start by acknowledging and owning up to our many sins.

Paul called himself "the worst of sinners" (1 Timothy 1:16). He wasn't paralyzed by condemnation. He was exalting God's grace by recognizing his own unworthiness and sin as he marveled at the mercy of God.

Every one of us can honestly claim that "worst of sinners" title. No, it isn't specially reserved for the Adolf Hitlers, Timothy McVeighs, and Osama bin Ladens of the world. William Law writes, "We may justly condemn ourselves as the greatest sinners we know because we know more of the folly of our own heart than we do of other people's."[9]

So admit you're the worst sinner you know. Admit you're unworthy and deserve to be condemned. But don't stop there! Move on to rejoicing in the Savior who came to save the worst of sinners. Lay down the luggage of condemnation and kneel down in worship at the feet of Him who bore your sins. Cry tears of amazement.

And confess with Paul: "I was shown mercy so that in me, the worst of sinners, Christ Jesus might display his unlimited patience as an example for those who would believe on him and receive eternal life" (1 Timothy 1:16).

Five

WHAT YOU FEEL
vs. WHAT IS REAL

Basing Your Faith in
Christ's Finished Work at the Cross

"HAVE YOU REALIZED," preacher David Martyn Lloyd-Jones once observed, "that most of your unhappiness in life is due to the fact that you are listening to yourself instead of talking to yourself?"[10]

I agree. Let me explain what Mr. Lloyd-Jones means by "listening to yourself." If you're anything like me, there's a good chance you do it every day. You know the routine. Every morning the alarm clock erupts, demanding attention.

Make it stop…make it stop! You hit the "snooze" button.

A precious eight minutes of floating, timeless oblivion pass. Then the grating alarm starts again. You open your eyes and the "listening" begins.

Today is…Thursday. Oh, no, you have the sales meeting! You're better off curling up here for the day.

You should exercise. Oooh, the back is sore, forget it.

Two feet are thrown over the side of the bed. The voice keeps talking.

Yesterday…what was it? Oh, that new noise from the car. Great. Life is just one big broken, whirring mess of…and you need to balance the checkbook.

As your bare feet hit the cold bathroom floor, the voice picks up its pace.

What did Laura mean by that comment? Was she being sarcastic? Can't anyone in this family learn to put the toothpaste back?

This weekend will be so busy. You've got so much to do today. You should pray. You don't have time to pray. You didn't pray yesterday.

This mirror needs to be cleaned. Shouldn't have watched that show last night. Wow! I need a haircut.

Soon.

God feels kind of distant?

Oh, I feel so drained….

Can you relate? On a daily basis we're faced with two simple choices. We can either *listen* to ourselves and our constantly changing feelings about our circumstances, or we can *talk* to ourselves about the unchanging truth of who God is and what He's accomplished for us at the cross.

Far too often we choose to passively listen to ourselves. We sit back and let our view of God and life be shaped by our constantly shifting feelings about our ever-changing circumstances. Life is busy. Often hard. Full of distractions. And before a morning cup of coffee, our passive listening can take us on a roller-coaster ride as we review a hundred different topics and experience a dozen varied emotions.

Is it any wonder we're so often unhappy? We're listening to ourselves. We need to start talking to ourselves instead.

BAD ADVICE

In the last two chapters, we learned about legalism and condemnation. But before you can make real progress against them or any other sin, you need to understand the importance of what happens inside your head. The cross centered life starts with biblical thinking. Are you going to build your life on what you feel or on what is real?

Scottish theologian Sinclair Ferguson has noted,

"The evangelical orientation is inward and subjective. We are far better at looking inward than we are at looking outward. Instead, we need to expend our energies admiring, exploring, expositing, and extolling Jesus Christ."[11] What that means is that we're focused on ourselves and our own feelings.

Think about this. How often in a typical day do you take an internal inventory in an effort to evaluate how you're doing? How often do you assess a situation by examining how you feel about it? How often do you make mental reference to how you feel, as opposed to what you know?

Or, most important, to what Scripture teaches? In other words, how often do you "follow your heart"?

"We think with our feelings,"[12] Ferguson has said. It's true. We allow our feelings to guide our thinking, and we shouldn't. Emotions are a wonderful gift from God. And our relationship with God should bring to our lives strong godly affections. However, our emotions shouldn't be vested with final authority. This should be reserved for God's Word alone.

THE POWER OF LOOKING OUTWARD

Not long ago, in the final stages of preparing my message for the next morning, I knocked a mug of hot coffee directly onto the keyboard of my laptop computer. The machine gasped out a mournful "fffftttt!" and the screen went blank.

In an instant of clumsiness, I had destroyed my computer, vaporized my sermon notes, and added hours to my preparation time. Frozen in disbelief, I stared dumbfounded at the empty screen. The keyboard took on the look of a small tropical swamp, its keys poking out of the steaming coffee like lily pads.

I wish I could say I trusted God in that moment. Nope. Instead I let out an angry, bloodcurdling "Nooooooo!!" Then I picked my chair a few inches up off the floor and slammed it back down.

Instantly I was convicted. God had been revealing a pattern of complaint in my heart and once again I'd sinned. Instead of trusting Him, instead of acknowledging that He was sovereign and I was just His servant, I'd yelled an angry, defiant "No!" to heaven and slammed my chair.

Almost immediately, the voice of my own feelings started to speak.

How could God allow this? Why is this happening? Oh, great—now you're sinning! You're a pastor? You're going to try and preach to others after that pitiful display of anger? How can you ask God to help you prepare now? This stinks. Look at what you've done!

I'm grateful that God helped me stop listening in that moment. I knew I needed to talk to myself. And because I knew I needed help, I went upstairs and involved my wife, Carolyn. First, she gently helped me see the sin that had caused my outburst. Then together, we reviewed the gospel.

Later, I went downstairs and began the tedious process of reassembling my message. But now I was talking to myself. "Your sin of anger has been atoned for by another. Jesus died for that sin. Jesus, the one who passed every test, who was tempted in every way but never sinned. He stood in your place and He was punished in your place. God has forgiven you and He's going to help you prepare and preach this message, not because you're sinless but because He is merciful!"

By God's grace I was able to turn away from what I felt and live in the good of what was true and unchanging—God's grace to me through the cross. And, thankfully, the sermon turned out fine.

My computer didn't do so well, but that's another story!

EXTOLLING JESUS CHRIST

Martin Luther wrote, "[The righteousness of Christ] is entirely outside and above us."[13] That's why we need to stop looking inward and look outward at the work of Christ on our behalf. As Sinclair Ferguson stated, we should "expend our energies admiring, exploring, expositing, and extolling Jesus Christ."[14]

And we can do this regardless of how we feel, because the gospel exists independently of us. The purpose of the gospel, as Knox Chamblin has noted, is to "proclaim saving events,"[15] and its events remain completely unaffected by whatever is agitating our emotions. The gospel is objective.

That which is subjective changes regularly, like shifting sand. But that which is objective is built on the solid rock of the gospel. When we look inward, we live by the subjective, the temporal, the ever-changing, the unreliable, the likely-to-be-false. When we look outward, to the gospel, we live by the objective, the never changing, that which is perfectly reliable and always completely true.

Our life in Christ is based on objective truth, and the chief truth among the innumerable glorious truths of Scripture is that Jesus died for your sins. That's the heart of the gospel.

Thus the point of this chapter is a simple one: Don't listen to yourself; talk to yourself! Begin your day and at numerous points throughout the day expend your energies "admiring, exploring, expositing, and extolling Jesus Christ."

This is what cross centered living is all about. And it will make that daily encounter with the alarm clock a lot more bearable.

Six

THE CROSS CENTERED DAY

Practical Ways to Center Every Day around the Cross

WE HUMANS ARE CREATURES OF HABIT, aren't we? And our habits reflect our true selves—we all build our daily lives around our priorities and passions.

Visit the same coffee shop a few mornings in a row and you'll see what I'm talking about. Each day the same people repeat the same routine, over and over. That cup of coffee and the caffeine boost it provides is an integral part of each day. For many people, that's how they start off right.

You might not be a coffee drinker, but I'm sure you

have your own daily rituals. Reading the sports page of the *Washington Post* each day became one of mine. To this very moment, I count it a good day when I can sit down, read my favorite columnists, and get the latest scores and stats.

Add eating chocolate to the routine and it becomes a *very* good day!

We make time for what we truly value. We build habits and routines around the things that really matter to us. This is an important principle to understand as we seek to build our lives around the gospel. Do you want a cross centered life?

A cross centered life is made up of cross centered days.

PREACH TO YOURSELF

Reminding ourselves of the gospel is the most important daily habit we can establish. If the gospel is the most vital news in the world, and if salvation by grace is the defining truth of our existence, we should create ways to immerse ourselves in these truths every day. No days off allowed.

In his book *The Discipline of Grace*, Jerry Bridges calls this "preaching the gospel to yourself."[16] Don't worry— even if you don't consider yourself a public speaker, you can do this. Your audience is your own heart. And the message is simple: Christ died for your sins.

"To preach the gospel to yourself," Bridges explains, "means that you continually face up to your own sinfulness and then flee to Jesus through faith in His shed blood and righteous life."[17]

It's a matter of sitting yourself down, grabbing your own attention, and saying, "Hey, self, listen up! This is what matters most: You're forgiven! You have hope! Your hope is based on the sacrifice of Jesus. So let's not view this day any other way. Let this day be governed by this *one defining truth*."

PASSION IN THE MIDST OF DRIZZLE

But let's be practical. It's one thing to get excited when you hear an inspiring sermon or read a book. How do you maintain your cross centeredness in the midst of a busy schedule amid the demands of work and family?

John Stott, author and pastor, compares the cross to a blazing bonfire. If we want the flame in our heart to be kept alive, we have to keep coming back to the source. "The cross is the blazing fire at which the flame of our love is kindled," he writes, "but we have to get near enough *to it* for its sparks to fall on us."[18]

How do you keep the flame of gospel passion burning brightly in the drizzle of real life? Let me share five very simple ways I've found that help me draw near to the "sparks" of the cross each day.

1. MEMORIZE THE GOSPEL

The Bible refers to memorizing Scripture as storing up His Word in our hearts (Psalm 119:11). I love that picture. God wants us to tuck His promises into our hearts so that, no matter where we are or what we're doing, we can pull them out and be strengthened by their truth.

You might not think you're good at memorizing Scripture. That's okay. Don't give up. Work at it. God isn't keeping score. Even if it takes you longer than someone else, it's worth the effort.

And if you're already memorizing Scripture, practice what my friend Mike Bullmore calls "strategic scripture memory." Start with the gospel. All God's promises and commands are precious, but those verses that tell us of the Son of God who gave His life in our place are the most precious of all. Since you have to begin somewhere, why not start with the central message of the Bible?

Having these verses instantly accessible is so helpful. For example, if you find yourself losing perspective at a difficult point in the day, reach into your memory and pull out 2 Corinthians 5:21: "For our sake he made him to be sin who knew no sin, so that in him we might become the righteousness of God" (ESV).

Does that put things in a new light? God has addressed our most serious problem: sin and judgment. This perspective has a transforming effect in the midst of the daily troubles and inconveniences of life.

Or what if you're struggling with condemnation over sin you've repented of and turned away from? Pull out Romans 8:31–34:

> If God is for us, who can be against us? He who did not spare his own Son but gave him up for us all, how will he not also with him graciously give us all things? Who shall bring any charge against God's elect? It is God who justifies. Who is to condemn? Christ Jesus is the one who died—more than that, who was raised—who is at the right hand of God, who indeed is interceding for us. (ESV)

God has given us these passages to help us preach to ourselves! Here are more key passages that speak of God's work of salvation through the cross. You're probably familiar with some or all of these, but let me encourage you to read and reflect on them again. I'm providing them here in the English Standard Version of the Bible. This is the version I use and recommend.

Isaiah 53:3—6

He was despised and rejected by men; a man of
sorrows, and acquainted with grief; and as one
from whom men hide their faces he was
despised, and we esteemed him not. Surely he
has borne our griefs and carried our sorrows; yet
we esteemed him stricken, smitten by God, and
afflicted. But he was wounded for our transgressions; he was crushed for our iniquities; upon
him was the chastisement that brought us peace,
and with his stripes we are healed. All we like
sheep have gone astray; we have turned every
one to his own way; and the Lord has laid on
him the iniquity of us all.

Romans 3:23—26

For all have sinned and fall short of the glory of
God, and are justified by his grace as a gift,
through the redemption that is in Christ Jesus,
whom God put forward as a propitiation by his
blood, to be received by faith. This was to show
God's righteousness, because in his divine forbearance he had passed over former sins. It was
to show his righteousness at the present time, so

that he might be just and the justifier of the one who has faith in Jesus.

Romans 5:6–11

For while we were still weak, at the right time Christ died for the ungodly. For one will scarcely die for a righteous person—though perhaps for a good person one would dare even to die—but God shows his love for us in that while we were still sinners, Christ died for us. Since, therefore, we have now been justified by his blood, much more shall we be saved by him from the wrath of God. For if while we were enemies we were reconciled to God by the death of his Son, much more, now that we are reconciled, shall we be saved by his life. More than that, we also rejoice in God through our Lord Jesus Christ, through whom we have now received reconciliation.

Romans 8:32–39

He who did not spare his own Son but gave him up for us all, how will he not also with him graciously give us all things? Who shall bring any charge against God's elect? It is God who justifies.

Who is to condemn? Christ Jesus is the one who died—more than that, who was raised—who is at the right hand of God, who indeed is interceding for us. Who shall separate us from the love of Christ? Shall tribulation, or distress, or persecution, or famine, or nakedness, or danger, or sword?

No, in all these things we are more than conquerors through him who loved us. For I am sure that neither death nor life, nor angels nor rulers, nor things present nor things to come, nor powers, nor height nor depth, nor anything else in all creation, will be able to separate us from the love of God in Christ Jesus our Lord.

1 Corinthians 15:3–4, ESV

For I delivered to you as of first importance what I also received: that Christ died for our sins in accordance with the Scriptures, that he was buried, that he was raised on the third day in accordance with the Scriptures.

2 Corinthians 5:21, ESV

For our sake he made him to be sin who knew no sin, so that in him we might become the righteousness of God.

Galatians 2:21, ESV

I do not nullify the grace of God, for if justification were through the law, then Christ died for no purpose.

2. PRAY THE GOSPEL

The gospel should be at the center of your prayer life. The gospel makes it possible for us to approach God. The gospel gives us the confidence to pray boldly—we're accepted in God's beloved Son.

There's nothing complicated about this. To pray the gospel, simply begin by thanking God for the blessing of eternal life, purchased through the death of His Son. Acknowledge that Christ's work on the cross is what makes your very prayer possible.

Thank Him that, because Jesus bore God's wrath for sin, you will never be separated from God's love. Thank Him that, because of the cross, you are reconciled to God and have been given the Holy Spirit to dwell in you, lead you, guide you, and empower you to resist sin and serve God. Then ask God to bless you graciously with all that you need to obey and glorify Him.

We come by the cross, we stand confidently because of the cross, we have the right to ask boldly because of the cross. The gospel should be woven in throughout our praise, our petition, and our intercession.

3. SING THE GOSPEL

I'm no singer (ask my friends), but I love to sing about the cross. A Christian's heart should be brimming every day with the song of Calvary. This is another opportunity to be strategic. There are countless worship CDs available, but it's important to choose ones that draw our attention to the amazing truth of what God has done on our behalf. Not all worship songs are created equal. Many today are man centered, not cross centered. They focus more on what we need, or what we want God to do, than on what Jesus has already done.

I have to admit I'm spoiled when it comes to great cross centered worship songs. Some of my friends are very gifted songwriters who create incredible, contemporary worship songs that are filled with the gospel. (You can find out more about these songs and albums at www.sovereigngraceministries.org.)

Wherever you find it, please make cross centered worship a regular part of your daily routine. If like me you can't play an instrument, worship to recorded music. There is no better way to start each day than to employ songs and hymns that speak of the cross with clarity and power.

Let me share a few of my favorites. Please don't skip or rush through them as you read. Take these in slowly; read them out loud. First, let the words of this hymn by Horatius Bonar echo through your soul:

> 'Twas I that shed the sacred Blood,
> I nailed him to the Tree,
> I crucified the Christ of God;
> I joined the mockery.
> And of that shouting multitude
> I feel that I am one;
> And in that din of voices rude
> I recognize my own.
> Around the Cross the throng I see
> That mock the Sufferer's groan;
> Yet still my voice it seems to be,
> As if I mocked alone.[19]

Do you feel the effect these rich words can have on you? Here's another classic by John Newton:

In evil long I took delight
Unawed by shame or fear;
Till a new object struck my sight
And stopped my wild career.
I saw one hanging on a tree
In agonies and blood;
Who fixed his languid eyes on me
As near his cross I stood.
Sure never till my latest breath
Can I forget that look;
It seemed to charge me with his death
Though not a word he spoke.
My conscience felt and owned the guilt
And plunged me in despair;
I saw my sins his blood had spilt
And helped to nail him there.
Alas, I knew not what I did
But now my tears are vain;
Where shall my trembling soul be hid?
For I the Lord have slain.
A second look he gave which said
"I freely all forgive;
This blood is for thy ransom paid
I died that thou mayest live."

Thus while his death my sin displays
In all its blackest hue;
Such is the mystery of grace,
It seals my pardon too.
With pleasing grief and mournful joy
My spirit now is filled;
That I should such a life destroy
Yet live by him I killed.[20]

Hymns like these, and many contemporary worship choruses as well, *if they are centered on the cross*, can help you make the gospel the sound track of your day.

4. REVIEW HOW THE GOSPEL HAS CHANGED YOU

Many people today want to forget the past. The mistakes they've made and the sins they've committed aren't subjects they like to revisit. But for Christians, one of the best ways we can draw near the blazing fire of the cross is to remember the past. It should remind us of how marvelous God's salvation really is.

The apostle Paul was committed to remembering what he once was because that memory magnified God's grace. "Even though I was once a blasphemer and a persecutor and a violent man, I was shown mercy" (1 Timothy 1:13). Though written some thirty years after his conversion, Paul remembered vividly and specifically his many sins prior to conversion. Knox Chamblin writes, "Vital to Paul's effectiveness as an apostle is that he never forgets his day as a persecutor....An ongoing awareness of grace reminds Paul of the appalling sin from which he has been delivered; an ongoing awareness of sin keeps him dependent on grace."[21]

It's vital for us never to forget as well. We need to follow Paul's example. We can all say, "I was once a _____" and fill in our own descriptions of our sinful state. And we don't need a dramatic testimony to do so. Even if your story doesn't involve drugs or immorality, it is still a miracle of God's grace. You didn't write it by yourself. God intervened. God changed your heart. God saved you.

Take time to think about all that. Reflect on it daily. I would also encourage you to write out your testimony in a page or two. And don't just write "I asked Jesus into my heart." Really spell out the heart of the gospel and how the blood of Christ, shed for the sins of the world, came to apply to you personally. Be specific about the fact that God is holy and you were an object of His wrath. Identify the sin in which you were lost. Explain how God saved you and changed your life for His glory.

This will edify and encourage you, and prepare you

to share both your personal testimony and the truth of the gospel with others.

5. STUDY THE GOSPEL

To grow in your *passion* for what Jesus has done, increase your *understanding* of what He has done.

Never be content with your current grasp of the gospel. The gospel is life-permeating, world-altering, universe-changing truth. It has more facets than any diamond. Its depths man will never exhaust.

So let me share some practical recommendations for making the gospel an ongoing life-study.

- Camp out in the books of Romans and Galatians. Author John Stott, among others, has written excellent commentaries on both to assist you in your study.
- Don't be afraid of technical theological terms. Take the time to learn the meaning of such words as *atonement, substitution, propitiation, justification, redemption, reconciliation,* and *salvation.* If you're looking for a guide, *The Atonement* by Leon Morris[22] explains each of these words in detail. Understanding them will better help you appreciate and marvel at what God has done.

- Here's a New Year's resolution that is truly worthwhile. Make it an annual goal to read at least one new book on the cross, and to reread a second book on the cross. The list I provide below will give you some great ones to start with.

The Cross of Christ by John Stott. A personal favorite. Stott says of the Savior, "It was by his death that he wished above all else to be remembered."[23] This book won't let you forget.

The Discipline of Grace by Jerry Bridges.[24] Another personal favorite. The first three chapters of this book in particular are worth reading and rereading for the rest of your life.

The Power of the Cross of Christ by Charles Spurgeon.[25] My historical hero exhorts us to "abide hard by the cross and search the mystery of his wounds."[26] There is no better human guide for this holy search.

The Cross & Christian Ministry by D. A. Carson.[27] For pastors this is a must-read. I'm indebted to Dr. Carson for this book. It has defined effective pastoral ministry for me, and it will do the same for you.

- Do you have a daily commute, or another regular time when you can listen to a tape? Get ahold of cross centered preaching that you can benefit from—visit www.sovereigngraceministries.org for a list of tapes on the cross.
- Read your whole Bible with your eyes peeled for the gospel. It has been noted that every passage of Scripture—whether it's in the Old or New Testament—either predicts, prepares for, reflects, or results from the work of Christ. As you read Scripture in your daily devotions, identify which category each passage fits into. The Old Testament in particular will come alive as you see it pointing to the coming Savior.

YOU CAN'T DO THIS ON YOUR OWN

I hope these five practical recommendations have given you a clearer understanding of what it means to make every day a day centered on the cross. But as we think about all these activities, it's vital to remember that we can't do this on our own. We need God's Spirit to light the truths of the cross within our hearts. This is true at the moment our hearts are regenerated and it's true every day of our Christian lives.

True conversion requires that God open our spiritual

eyes to the truth of the gospel. In a similar way, every time you look with fresh amazement at the cross of Christ, another miracle is taking place. You are receiving a supernatural gift, the gift of illumination. You are seeing something to which you would be completely blind were the Spirit of God not at that moment granting you spiritual sight. Dr. Don Carson writes:

> There has not only been an objective, public act of divine self-disclosure in the crucifixion of God's own Son, but there must be a private work of God by His Spirit, in the mind and heart of the individual. If we should express unqualified gratitude to God for the gift of his Son, we should express no less gratitude for the gift of the Spirit who enables us to grasp the gospel of His Son…Unless the Spirit enlightens us, God's thoughts will remain deeply alien to us.[28]

Each time we memorize, pray, sing, review, or study the gospel we must ask the Holy Spirit to open our eyes and bring the gospel alive to us again. He is quick to hear and faithful to answer. But His help must be actively sought.

Because of the empowering grace of God's Spirit, I've

been drawing near the blaze of the cross day after day for many years now. Don't get me wrong. I haven't done it perfectly, and there have been many days when my heart isn't as passionate as it should be. But I can honestly say that my appreciation of and passion for the gospel has been growing steadily.

The suggestions I've made in this chapter have been invaluable to me in that growing process. Through them the sparks from the blazing fire of the cross have fallen on me many, many times, and my own zeal has burned brighter and brighter.

If God can do this in my life, He can do the same for you. Draw near the blaze every day.

Build a cross centered life, one day at a time.

Seven

NEVER MOVE ON

Put This Book on a Shelf,
but Not Its Message!

I WAS SMOKING POT THE FIRST TIME I heard the gospel. People often ask me why I'm so confident in God's grace. I explain that my understanding of Scripture and my own conversion experience leave me with no other explanation.

God came looking for me.

I'm a Christian because God showed mercy, not because I was worthy or wanting to be saved. No, I wasn't searching for God. I was stoned.

It was 1972. I was sitting in my bedroom smoking a joint when my friend Bob began to share the simple story of Jesus dying for my sins. I'd grown up in the Catholic church and had never heard the gospel.

But that night as I listened, God revealed Himself and regenerated my heart. I believed. The cross was for *me*. Jesus was *my* savior. The worst of sinners, in the midst of his sin, was born again.

That was thirty years ago.

A lot has changed. The long hair has all fallen out. I'm a grandfather. In the past two years I've celebrated my twenty-fifth wedding anniversary and my twenty-fifth year as a pastor.

I've learned a lot since then, too. At the time, I literally knew nothing of God or His Word. I'd never cracked open a Bible. But from the day of my conversion I couldn't get enough of Scripture or Christian books. Not long after my conversion, I got a job at a Christian bookstore just so I could read as much as possible.

My love for books hasn't abated. Today the walls of my office at the church are lined with books from floor to ceiling. Sometimes in the midst of my daily responsibilities I'll look up at them, amazed at the difference they've made in my life.

The thousands of titles are a striking visual reminder of the many ideas and messages—good and not-so-good—that have vied for my attention over the years. Most of my collection comprises classic books written hundreds of years ago by men like Charles Spurgeon, Jonathan Edwards, and the Puritans. But I also have many books written more recently.

Some are better than others. I could take you to some that represent Christian fads of the past thirty years. At the time, their innovative ideas for personal growth and effective ministry were all the rage. Now they're forgotten.

I keep them because I want a sobering reminder, constantly close to me, of all the off-center messages that might tempt me to move on from the *one message that matters*—the gospel.

David Prior said it best in one of my favorite quotes: "We never move on from the cross, only into a more profound understanding of the cross."[29] A lot has changed since I first trusted in Christ, but a lot has stayed the same. I'm grateful to say that what matters the most has remained the same. *The cross is still at the center.*

I've come a long way since I heard the gospel in a drug-induced high. I've traveled many miles in this journey of faith. But by His grace I've never moved on from the cross of Jesus Christ. And I never want to.

IT REALLY IS ENOUGH

Here we are at the final chapter of this small book. Once you've finished just a few more pages you'll be done, and you'll place this volume on a bookshelf of your own. Maybe one day in the future you'll pull it out to review a quote or flip through a chapter or two. Or maybe you'll never touch it again.

Don't worry, I won't mind if my book winds up in a forgotten corner of a bookshelf, collecting dust. But I do hope that the message of this book is one you'll *never* put on a shelf.

You may forget this book and its author, but *never let the message of the cross slide into second or third place in your life. Never lay it aside. Never move on.*

I can hear you asking, "But don't I need more than that?" In one sense the answer is no. Nothing else is of equal importance. The message of the cross is the Christian's hope, confidence, and assurance. Heaven will be spent marveling at the work of Christ, the God-Man who suffered in the place of us sinners.

And yet, in another sense the answer is yes, you do need more. You've been saved to grow, to serve in a local church, to do good works and to glorify God. But the "more" that you need as a follower of Christ won't be found apart from the cross. The gospel isn't one class among many that you'll attend during your life as a Christian—the gospel is the whole building that all the classes take place in!

Rightly approached, all the topics you'll study and

focus on as a believer will be offered to you "within the walls" of the glorious gospel.

"The Spirit does not take his pupils beyond the cross," writes J. Knox Chamblin, "but ever more deeply into it."[30]

YEAH, BUT WHAT ABOUT...

Name the area of the Christian life that you want to learn about or that you want to grow in. The Old Testament? The end times? Do you want to grow in holiness or the practice of prayer? To become a better husband, wife, or parent? None of these can be rightly understood apart from God's grace through Jesus' death. They, and indeed all topics, should be studied through the lens of the gospel.

Let me share a few specific examples of what it means to study the following areas through this lens.

1. The Old Testament

Some people are scared of the Old Testament. They find it confusing and hard to understand. Others are fascinated with it for the wrong reasons.

Only the person who understands that the cross is the center of all human history can understand the Old

Testament. Through the lens of the gospel, the Bible truly becomes one book telling one story: the story of sinful man, a holy God, and His plan of salvation through the substitution of Himself for His people.

To be a true student of the ancient books of Scripture, we don't move on from the gospel. Quite the contrary! Everything in the Old Testament points toward Jesus Christ and enriches our understanding of the cross (see Luke 24:27).

The drama of redemption begins in the Garden in Genesis 3 and continues to unfold throughout the Old Testament until it reaches its climax at the cross. All along the way, the Divine Author prepares us for Calvary: The symbolism of the sacrificial system, the strictness of the law, the repeated failures of man, and the steadfast faithfulness of God—all this and more deepens our amazement at the cross.

2. The End Times

In the past hundred years, much has been written about the last days and the final return of Christ. The study of the end times is called eschatology. Because it provides limitless possibilities to the human imagination, eschatology has become a popular subject for novelists, playing to the conspiracy-theory tendencies in modern man.

Please don't misunderstand. What we believe about Christ's return is important. But what's sad is the inordinate amount of attention and energy given to the details of that return, balanced against the distinct lack of focus on the saving work of the cross that should stand at the very center of any such discussion.

Regardless of your personal opinion about the Rapture, or the Millennium, it's undeniable that in Scripture the work of Christ at Calvary still takes center stage. His Second Coming is the culmination of the victory He accomplished over death and hell at the cross.

Jesus did not instruct his disciples to concern themselves with the details of when and where. They were to watch and pray, but their primary preoccupation was to be *exulting in and proclaiming the good news of His death and resurrection.*

Because of the cross the end is already written! Jesus is victorious! All those who trust in Him have eternal life! Satan is defeated! No force on earth, no agonies of persecution, can snatch away from Him those He died to save. Nothing can separate them from His love.

3. Prayer

Effective prayer is prayer saturated in the gospel. To learn to pray you must become familiar with the Bible's teaching on prayer. You'll want to pray with other godly Christians and learn from their example. But again, you don't move on from the cross to go deeper into prayer. Ultimately, all effective prayer is rooted in the cross.

Think about it. The gospel is the starting point of prayer. Without Christ's blood, you couldn't even approach God. Only in Jesus' righteousness are we invited to enter His presence.

There's no mantra we can learn, no catchphrase we can recite, that will move God's hand. We appeal to Him based on the person and work of His son. Jerry Bridges writes, "When we pray to God for His blessing, He does not examine our performance to see if we are worthy. Rather, He looks to see if we are trusting in the merit of His Son as our only hope for securing His blessing."[31]

Students of the school of prayer never graduate from the school of the gospel.

4. Holiness

Do you want to grow in personal holiness? Maybe there's a particular area of sin you battle that you want to overcome. Here's the temptation you'll face.

Your pride and sinfully self-sufficient nature will tell you, "Okay, this material about the gospel has been great.

But now it's time to put all that grace aside and get down to work. It's time to make some change happen and get holy!"

That's not going to work. Driven by legalistic fervor, you might appear to make progress; but it will be short-lived. Only grace sustains lasting change and sanctification. Through the cross we overcome not only the guilt of sin, but the power of sin as well. Because of the cross we can successfully battle and overcome sinful patterns and practices. The cross motivates us to be holy as our Father in heaven is holy. The gospel empowers our ongoing pursuit of sanctification.

5. Relationships

What about the practical stuff? Surely there comes a time when we move on from the gospel just a little, so we can focus on the everyday issues of our relationships with other people.

This is tempting to believe, but it's just not true. Regardless of your relationship to others, whether you're single or married, a husband or a wife, a father, a mother, or a grandparent, your faithfulness and effectiveness in your relationships are directly tied to your understanding of the cross.

Because of sin, relational conflict is inevitable. You'll

sin against others. They'll sin against you. You'll need to forbear with others. You'll need to forgive.

Your relationships with others must be based on your relationship to God through the cross. Ephesians 4:32 states, "Be kind and compassionate to one another, forgiving each other, just as in Christ God forgave you."

When I become bitter or unforgiving toward others, I'm assuming that the sins of others are more serious than my sins against God. The cross transforms my perspective. Through the cross I realize that no sin committed against me will ever be as serious as the innumerable sins I've committed against God. When we understand how much God has forgiven us, it's not difficult to forgive others.

God's been patient with me so I can be patient with others. God has forgiven me so I can forgive others. God's grace is changing me so I can trust that he can also change others.

There's so much more that can be said. This is just a brief introduction to the transforming effect of the cross on every one of our relationships. But the point is simple yet powerful.

If you're single, live a cross centered life. If you're married, build a cross centered marriage. If you have children, practice cross centered parenting. The "practical" stuff flows from the "central" stuff.

WHEN YOU SUFFER

In the five areas above, I've presented just a small sampling of how to view life through the lens of the gospel. No such study can be exhaustive, but it can provide a basic example of how to process and understand every subject through the gospel lens.

What I hope you see is that the cross centered life isn't just one option among many that God offers. It is *the* life that *every* Christian is called to.

But there's one additional aspect of life that we need to examine, and that is suffering. As Paul sat writing to Timothy from that cold dungeon, he spoke of his own suffering because he knew that, inevitably, Timothy would one day suffer, too.

So will we.

You might be facing trial and suffering right now. If not, it is inevitable that eventually you will. In his outstanding book *How Long, O Lord,* which examines suffering and evil, D. A. Carson writes, "The truth of the matter is all we have to do is live long enough and we will suffer."[32]

Sometimes our suffering will mean simply persevering through a prolonged season that is not to our liking. At other times, our suffering may be acute and severe. In each case, the message of the gospel provides the ultimate source of hope and comfort.

Too many of us are not prepared theologically for suffering. So when we do suffer, instead of trusting God we complain. We charge Him. We demand that He explain himself. I'm not minimizing the difficulty and agony of suffering. Nor do I pretend to understand it completely. Scripture teaches there is a divine purpose for suffering, but there will always be an element of mystery.

I can't fully grasp the meaning or purpose of my suffering, but I can find true comfort from looking to the suffering of the only innocent and righteous one—our Savior. Again, D. A. Carson writes:

> In the darkest night of the soul, Christians have something to hold onto that Job never knew— we know Christ crucified. Christians have learned that when there seems to be no other evidence of God's love, they cannot escape the cross. "He who did not spare his own son but gave him up for us all—how will he not also, along with him, graciously give us all things?" (Romans 8:32).... When we suffer there will sometimes be mystery. Will there also be faith? Yes. If our attention is focused more on the cross and on the God of the cross than on the suffering itself.[33]

In real life, things do not always go just as we would like. Comfort in suffering can never be found by focusing endlessly on the suffering itself, for suffering always contains an element of impenetrable mystery. Hope and comfort and perseverance in the Christian life come from meditating on the cross and the God of the cross.

BETTER THAN I DESERVE

Ask me how I'm doing on any given day and you might be surprised by my response. I don't give the typical "I'm great" or "Fine, thanks!"

Instead I say, "Better than I deserve."

It catches people off guard. Many times non-Christians have argued with me, convinced that I suffer from low self-esteem.

But no—I just understand who I am and where I deserve to be. I deserve God's wrath. Honestly, I deserve to be in hell. But instead I'm God's child. I'm forgiven and loved by Him. I'm going to heaven.

I'm doing much better than I deserve!

That perspective fills me with joy even on days when things aren't going as I planned. We all face disappointments and difficult circumstances. Some of us experience deep pain and loss. But regardless of the situation, understanding the gospel lets us marvel at God's love.

ONLY YESTERDAY

I don't know what tomorrow holds, but I do know this: Because of the cross I'll be doing much better than I deserve. That's why, for the rest of my life, I want only to move deeper into the wonderful mystery of God's love for me.

The gospel isn't just for unbelievers. It's for Christians, too. "Every day of our Christian experience," writes Jerry Bridges, "should be a day of relating to God on the basis of His grace alone. We are not only saved by grace, but we also live by grace every day."[34]

This is why the gospel is truly the main thing. This is why it should always be at the center of our lives.

So even though this little book is over, don't put its precious truth on the shelf. May the truth that saved you always be the dearest truth of your life. As Martin Luther reportedly said, "I feel as if Jesus had died only yesterday." May the reality of Christ's death for you be that near your heart.

Never move on from it.

Jesus died for your sins. May your every day be lived by His grace alone. May you know the joy and peace of the cross centered life.

The publisher and author would love to hear your comments about this book. *Please contact us at:* www.bigchangemoments.com

NOTES

1. D. A. Carson, *The Cross & Christian Ministry: An Exposition of Passages from 1 Corinthians* (Grand Rapids, Mich.: Baker Books, 1993), 38.

2. Jerry Bridges, *The Discipline of Grace* (Colorado Springs, Col.: NavPress, 1994), 46.

3. John R. W. Stott, *Guard the Gospel* (Downers Grove, Ill.: InterVarsity Press, 1973), 22.

4. This bit of wisdom appears in many places; recently, it was quoted by U.S. Secretary of Education William J. Bennett, in an address to the National Press Club, Washington, D.C., 17 March 1985.

5. Carson, *Cross & Christian Ministry*, 26.

6. Thomas R. Schreiner, *The Law & Its Fulfillment: A Pauline Theology of Law* (Grand Rapids, Mich.: Baker Books, 1993), 15.

7. William S. Plumer, *The Grace of Christ* (Keyser:

Odem Publications, 1853), 195.

8. Sinclair B. Ferguson, *Know Your Christian Life* (Downers Grove, Ill.: InterVarsity Press, 1981), 73.

9. William Law, as quoted in Gary Thomas, *Seeking the Face of God* (Nashville, Tenn.: Thomas Nelson Publishers, 1994), 135.

10. David Martyn Lloyd-Jones, *Spiritual Depression: Its Causes and Cure* (Grand Rapids, Mich.: Wm. B. Eerdmans Publishing Company, 1965, reprinted 2001), 20.

11. Sinclair B. Ferguson, from a class in Systematic Theology, Reformed Theological Seminary, January 2001.

12. Sinclair B. Ferguson, *Deserted by God?* (Grand Rapids, Mich.: Baker Books, 1993), 24.

13. Martin Luther, edited by Jaroslav Jan Pelikan, Hilton C. Oswald and Helmut T. Lehmann, *Luther's Works, vol. 24: Sermons on the Gospel of St. John* (St. Louis, Mo.: Concordia Publishing House, 1999, c1961), chapters 14–16.

14. Sinclair B. Ferguson, from a class in Systematic Theology, Reformed Theological Seminary, January 2001.

15. J. Knox Chamblin, *Paul and the Self: Apostolic Teaching for Personal Wholeness* (Grand Rapids, Mich.: Baker Books, 1993), 26.

16. Bridges, *Discipline of Grace,* 45.

17. Ibid., 58.

18. From *What Christ Thinks of the Church,* revised and illustrated edition, Milton Keynes (Word UK; Wheaton, Ill.: Harold Shaw, 1990). First published 1958 (UK) and 1959 (US).

19. From "I See the Crowd in Pilate's Hall" by Horatius Bonar, 1856.

20. John Newton, "In Evil Long I Took Delight," *Olney Hymns, Book 2: On Occasional Subjects* (London, Eng.: W. Oliver, 1779).

21. Chamblin, *Paul and the Self,* n.p.

22. Leon Morris, *The Atonement: Its Meaning and Significance* (Downers Grove, Ill.: InterVarsity Press, 1983).

23. John R. W. Stott, *The Cross of Christ* (Downers Grove, Ill.: InterVarsity Press, 1986), 68.

24. Bridges, *Discipline of Grace,* 45.

25. Charles Spurgeon, *The Power of the Cross,* compiled and edited by Lance Wubbels (Lynwood, Wash.:Emerald Books, 1995).

26. Charles Spurgeon, *Morning and Evening* (Peabody, Mass.: Hendrickson Publishers, 1991), 8.

27. Carson, *The Cross & Christian Ministry.*

28. Ibid., 52.

29. David Prior, *Message of 1 Corinthians: Life in the*

Local Church (Downers Grove, Ill.: InterVarsity Press, 1985), 51.

30. Chamblin, *Paul and the Self,* 117.

31. Bridges, *Discipline of Grace,* 19.

32. D. A. Carson, *How Long, O Lord?* (Grand Rapids, Mich.: Baker Books, 1990).

33. Ibid., 191.

34. Bridges, *Discipline of Grace,* 18.

More Materials by **C.J. Mahaney**
from Sovereign Grace Ministries

Songs for the Cross Centered Life
Here is a worship recording inspired by the book you hold in your hands. In the book, C.J. encourages us to use cross centered worship music every day to help keep our lives focused on the main thing. In this CD you will find 14 songs, featuring a variety of styles and approaches, with each song drawing the listener deeper into the endless glories of the cross of Christ.

Christ and Him Crucified
This collection of gripping, passionate messages—the basis of C.J. Mahaney's book, *Christ Our Mediator*—explores three interwoven aspects of Christ's death for the salvation of sinners. Jesus is the Mediator who bore God's full wrath. He is the substitutionary sacrifice who hung on the cross utterly alone. He is the forsaken one who made peace between God and men. Listen, and be changed by the gospel…again.

Humility (True Greatness)
What does it mean to be great? What does it mean to be humble? From the ancient Israelites to the brothers James and John, who wished to be the greatest among Jesus' disciples, this two-message series unpacks essential biblical teachings on pride and humility, and offers a highly practical road map to personal change. True greatness? True humility? They're the same thing.

In the World but Not of the World
God's word clearly warns us not to love the world or anything in it. What does obedience to this command look like for Christians in the 21st century? This six-message audio series offers clear, encouraging guidance in the areas of media, music, and modesty, helping you to steer a steady course between the twin dangers of legalism and license. C.J. Mahaney, Joshua Harris, and Bob Kauflin deliver two messages each.

These and many other helpful materials are available at the Sovereign Grace Ministries website. Articles, streaming media, worship music, and sermon notes from C.J. Mahaney and others may be found at **www.SovereignGraceMinistries.org**